Buddhism in 10 Steps

A practical and easy to understand
introduction to Buddhism for beginners

By Alan Peto
&
Sanathavihari Bhikkhu

Cover design and book layout by Alan Peto
Interior photos by Truthseeker08 on Pixabay (CC0 license)

ISBN: 9798409613723 (Paperback)

First Paperback Edition - February 2022
Published by Alan Peto

Get the PDF version of this book:
https://alanpeto.com/books/buddhism-10-steps/

"One is one's own protector.
What other protector could there be?

One is one's own refuge.
Therefore, one should control oneself
as a merchant controls a noble steed."

~ The Buddha

Contents

Welcome

Buddhism is a major worldwide religion with over half a billion followers which continues to gain the interest of people around the world.

Because those who are exploring or new to Buddhism can be inundated with too many resources, books, videos, and viewpoints, we felt a practical and easy-to-understand introduction to Buddhism would be beneficial to start you out correctly in your journey as a Buddhist layperson.

As someone new to Buddhism, we have centered this book around that fact, rather than explaining Buddhism at a scholarly or monastic level.

Inside this purposely short book, we will introduce you to several fundamental Buddhist teachings, concepts, and practices to give you a solid foundation.

We encourage you to explore and find a Buddhist temple near you where you can follow the guidance of Buddhist monastics and engage with the Buddhist community. If you do not have a temple near you, many are now providing online services and classes you can attend.

Welcome to the wonderful world of Buddhism and we wish you much merit in your practice!

~ Alan Peto & Sanathavihari Bhikkhu

Buddhism is Everything

By Venerable Sanathavihari Bhikkhu

What is Buddhism? Is it a religion, philosophy, or a way of life?

Like many of you I also had similar questions about "what is Buddhism?" So, I started off by reading many books on Buddhism, asking my Buddhist friends, and going to visit Buddhist centers.

On my journey to find out what Buddhism "is," I was amazed to learn how the many different Buddhist traditions defined Buddhism, and how Buddhist practice can be varied with each individual.

Then it occurred to me, Buddhism is *everything*. Everything in the sense that it cannot be relegated to a convenient conceptual box. Buddhism is a system, method, teaching, and practice that pervades every single dimension of life.

The teachings of the Buddha are not limited to sitting on a meditation cushion, in the monastery, on retreat, holidays, weddings, and funerals. The teachings of the Buddha are for every moment of life, from when we first wake up until the moment we fall asleep. And even in sleep Buddhism has something to offer us.

So, what does Buddhism have to offer us? Well, the Buddha said it is the end of all suffering and the supreme happiness of Nirvana. These might seem like quite lofty and idealistic goals. However, the same teachings that can help us achieve these somewhat fantastic goals also provide benefits in the here and now.

Whether you are interested in Buddhism because you are in search of transcendence or want to be a bit less of a jerk, the teachings of the Buddha can help in the mundane and the supermundane. You can find relief from suffering due to your online shopping order being late, to the extreme of losing a loved one. The solution to overcoming both are found in the same Buddhist practices.

I know that coming into Buddhism can seem overwhelming with the vast number of sutras, meditations, rituals, and customs. However, you can focus your mind and practice on what the Buddha said when he was asked for a concise version of his teachings:

"To avoid doing bad, to do good, and to develop the mind - this is the teaching of all the Buddhas."

Buddhism is Freedom

By Alan Peto

"Freedom" – The Buddha made it abundantly clear that what he taught was a matter of life and death. He could free us from the consequences of our own unskillful and unwholesome actions, but only if we were ready to hear his teachings and put in the effort.

This succinct message and mission of the Buddha can sometimes be lost in our distracted society that wants ideas that they agree with, things that make us feel better, and things that entertain us.

In Buddhist teachings, our mind is likened to a bull, ox, or monkey that is constantly going off in different directions based on the things *it* wants. You are unfortunately chained to this "bull" of a mind and dragged around endlessly, which is an unsatisfactory experience, to say the least. This "mind" that controls you is not the true nature of "you," and it wants to stay in charge, of course.

Yet, this is not how things need to be. The Buddha taught that our mind can be tamed so that we may re-discover our true nature that is free of ignorance, greed, and anger, known as *Nirvāṇa.*

He told us that realizing Nirvāṇa can only be accomplished in what we call the "human realm" (which you are in now) which is an incredibly rare opportunity. Therefore, we must not squander this chance to hear and practice the Dharma (the Buddha's teachings).

This message of liberation *and* urgency becomes more important to me every year I practice Buddhism. I have the choice of either resigning myself to being a compliant "prisoner" of my untamed mind, or I can work towards getting out of this self-imposed "prison" and rediscover my true nature.

Buddhism, the religion, is a well-honed sword that cuts through delusion and the ignorance of our untamed mind so we can become awakened to the truth, become an enlightened being, and realize our natural peaceful state of "Nirvāṇa" which is free of suffering and dissatisfaction.

This journey will not be easy and is filled with concepts and words that will be new to you but has the reward of freedom. Allow the teachings, practices, ceremonies, and traditions that have been refined for the past 2,600 years to guide you to enlightenment!

1 – What is Buddhism?

Buddhism provides the **liberating path** towards **freedom** *(Pāli: Nibbāna / Sanskrit: Nirvāṇa)* from unsatisfactoriness in life *(Pāli: Dukkha / Sanskrit: Duḥkha)*, which is a result of unwholesome karma, which gives rise to re-birth in the cycle of birth and death *(Saṃsāra)*.

1. **The Buddha's teachings explain the true nature of our existence and world, which is marked with Dukkha.** Because we are ignorant of the truth the Buddha taught *(Pāli: Dhamma / Sanskrit: Dharma)*, we believe Dukkha is our true nature or mental existence. This is because we are clouded to the truth of Dukkha's conditioned foundation which the Buddha said can be ended.

2. **The Buddha explained that unsatisfactoriness is rooted in the *Three Poisons (or Fires)*,** which are ignorance of the Dharma, the resulting greed, clinging, and craving to sensual pleasures, and anger and hatred when we are separated from pleasurable feelings, things, and perceptions.

3. **The *Three Poisons* give rise to unwholesome intentional volitional actions** *(Pāli: Kamma / Sanskrit: Karma)* **of the mind, body, and speech.** Karma is any intentional action that happens at every moment. However, it is not some otherworldly "judging force" but is rather the natural law of cause and effect where the results of actions can come to fruition immediately, in this lifetime, or future existences.

4. ***Karma* is what continues after death, connects all prior and future existences, and gives rise to new existences.** This is due to *Karma with outflows* (outflows are known as "fetters[1]" – which binds one in *Saṃsāra*).

---

[1] Fetters are mental beliefs or attitudes that bind one (like shackles) to the cycle of rebirth. While there are many fetters, the following are the most agreed upon and important to "cut off" in order to realize Nirvāṇa: 1) the belief in a permanent, unchanging, and independent "self", 2) doubt, which includes doubt about any of the Buddha's teachings (Dharma), and 3) attachment to rites and rituals [that do not lead to awakening].

5. **By becoming <u>awakened</u> to the truth (*Dharma*), one ends the delusion caused by our ignorance of the truth and can see the true nature of things – which is the conditioned, impermanent, ever-changing, and interconnected nature of our world.** This is the world that we previously viewed and interact with as unenlightened beings incorrectly due to our attachments and perceptions. When ignorance has been removed and one becomes awakened to the truth the Buddha taught, they have ended the unwholesome Karmic actions of greed and anger. Karma had been the force that prompted new existences to be created in the cycle of rebirth (*Saṃsāra*) which is unsatisfactory (*Dukkha*).

6. **One's true existence is free of the Three Poisons, Dukkha, and the Cycle of Rebirth, and is known as *Nirvāṇa*.** In this enlightened state, one no longer creates unskillful and unwholesome actions (*Karma*) that were leading to rebirth, which is unsatisfactory. They can now be in the world in their true natural state free of wrong perceptions, unskillful actions, and continued re-becoming in the cycle of rebirth.

The goal of all Buddhists is to become enlightened to the truth so they can free themselves from the cycle of rebirth (and the unsatisfactory nature of it) and realize their true natural peaceful state of Nirvāṇa.

2 – Who was the Buddha?

The historical Buddha was born **2,600 years ago** as **Siddhārtha Gautama** in the area where the modern-day country of Nepal is located, which is near modern-day India.

- Siddhārtha was born into a **life of luxury and privilege** but was **prevented** from **seeing real-life** by his father for fear he would become an ascetic/holy person. This was because it was predicted that Siddhārtha would be either a great ruler or a holy person. His father naturally wanted him to follow after him as a leader.

- He eventually **left** this life of luxury to become a holy person and learned many techniques from other teachers. However, none of these techniques led to the "truth" he was seeking.

- It was not until he nearly died after starving himself to attain higher levels of attainment that he resolved to follow the **"middle way"** of not going to extremes. He then resolved to meditate until he achieved awakening and realized enlightenment.

- He meditated for 49 days until he became enlightened, and was then known as the **Buddha**, which is the title of an enlightened teacher. He is the latest of many Buddhas who have existed in the past and is called **Shakyamuni Buddha** or **Gautama Buddha**. Shakya was his clan's name, and Shakyamuni is Sanskrit for "Sage of the Shakya." Shakyamuni Buddha is known as a **"Buddha of our era."** Each era has a single Buddha whose teachings (*Dharma*) we know and follow to become enlightened.

- The Buddha **taught** for roughly 45 years in the country known as **India**, establishing many monastic communities, followers, and giving teachings to numerous people.

- His foundational teachings are the **Four [Noble] Truths,** the **[Noble] Eightfold Path** (which is the fourth noble truth) leading to the freedom of *Nirvāṇa*, and **Dependent Origination**.

It's important to know that the title of "**Buddha**" is not restricted to Shakyamuni:

- There will be more Buddhas in the future when his teachings are lost in this world (the next Buddha of an era is known as **Maitreya**).

- There are "**solitary Buddhas**" (*Pratyekabuddhayāna*) which are enlightened beings that have awakened to the truth on their own (in an era *without* a Buddha) but do not enlighten others.

- In Mahāyāna Buddhism, all beings strive towards becoming a Buddha, even if that takes eons. There are countless Buddhas in other worlds and dimensions to aid one in this goal. For example, most Mahāyānists follow the path to enlightenment through *Amitābha Buddha* and his Western Pure Land. Pure Lands, also known as "Buddha Fields" (*buddhakṣetra*) are perfect environments where one can become more easily enlightened under a living Buddha. For example, when Shakyamuni was on this Earth, Vulture's Peak in India (where he gave many sermons) may be considered his Pure Land.

3 – What did the Buddha Teach?

The Buddha's teachings and mission are centered around one central theme: **the ending of unsatisfactoriness in our life** *(Pāli: Dukkha / Sanskrit: Duḥkha)*. His teachings help us to *end* the **delusion** of what we *believe* to be true about our self and reality by *transforming* **ignorance** through <u>wisdom</u>.

- Imagine you are driving your car on the wrong side of the road. This may result in a horrible accident for you or others. You are delusional because you think you are driving correctly. This delusion is caused by ignorance of how and why to drive correctly.

- When we view and interact with our world and self in a delusional way (which is unskillful and unwholesome) it is due to our ignorance of its true nature and the Buddha's teachings and path.

- Through Buddhist practice, one understands the truth of Dukkha, becomes enlightened, and realizes their true natural state of **Nirvāṇa.** This is accomplished by breaking down the belief in a permanent, unchanging, and independent "self" (ātman).

The Buddha identified *"**Three Marks of Existence**"* that permeate our reality:

1. **Impermanence:** No conditioned phenomena are permanent, and all are dependent on causes and conditions to exist (or cease). We call these two teachings *Impermanence* and *Dependent Origination.* This is a core principle in Buddhism because when we fundamentally understand that everything is impermanent, it liberates us from the false belief in a permanent "self."

2. **Suffering[2]:** Called *Duḥkha* or *Dukkha* in the Buddhist scriptures. Our reality and existence are unsatisfactory, even if we don't always perceive it this way. This suffering is caused by our belief that we are permanent, unchanging, and are not dependent on other things, which causes us to have attachments and cling to things. This in turn causes us to create actions (*Kamma/Karma*) that keep us trapped like prisoners in an endless cycle of rebirth (*Saṃsāra*).

3. **The illusion of Self:** Nothing is independent of other things to exist, and our belief that our 'body' and 'mind' makes us permanent and independent is false (known as *"anatman"* which means 'non-self' or 'not-self'). We are just a temporary grouping of things, known as the "Five Aggregates". The only thing that continues after we die is our actions (Karma).

Based on the Three Marks of Existence, the Buddha revealed the **true nature of our existence.** He explained that is Saṃsāra *is* Dukkha, which is rooted in the **Three Poisons** (also called the Three Fires) of our ignorance (and delusions), greed (desires), and anger (hatred).

- We fuel the Three Fires through our **sense organs** of the eyes, ears, nose, tongue, skin, and intellect ("manas") and how they react to **sense objects** of a visible object, sound, odor, taste, touch, and mental object (which are both material and immaterial).

- Saṃsāra is our **mundane existence**, which is full of impermanent and imperfect situations (Dukkha) created by our intentional actions (**Karma**). It is a **process of existence** that we flow through endlessly (rebirth). In contrast, **Nirvāṇa** is your true nature which is <u>absent</u> of the Three Poisons which is the root cause of Dukkha and continued re-birth.

---

[2] <u>There are three types of suffering</u>: 1) Suffering of "<u>Suffering</u>" *(Dukkha-dukkha)* due to the physical and emotional discomfort and pain we all experience as humans. 2) Suffering of "Change" *(Viparinama-dukkha)* due to our inability to accept the truth of impermanence and change, clinging to pleasurable experiences, and sadness when they pass. 3) Suffering of "<u>Existence</u>" *(Sankhara-dukkha)* due to the overall unsatisfactory nature of the arising of the Five Aggregates within Saṃsāra.

4 – What are the Four Noble Truths?

The Buddha's very **first sermon** was the **Four Noble Truths** called *"Turning the Wheel of the Dharma / Dhamma in Motion."* This sermon succinctly explained what "Buddhism" is and why we practice it. It is structured similar to the Buddha as a Doctor who explained your symptoms, illness, prognosis, and cure.

1. **The Truth of Dukkha** ("The Symptom"): You are suffering (*"Dukkha/ Duḥkha"*).

2. **The Cause of Dukkha** ("The Diagnosis"): Dukkha is caused by repeated "birth" due to clinging to the false belief in a permanent, unchanging, and independent "self", the resulting mental cravings of sensual pleasures *(Kāma)*, for existence *(Bhava)*, and for non-existence *(Vibhava)*, and the resulting karmic actions trapping one in rebirth. (*"Trishna / Taṇhā"*)

3. **The Truth of the End of Dukkha** ("The Prognosis"): There is a cure for Dukkha, which helps you achieve your true natural peaceful state known as *"Nibbāna / Nirvāṇa."*

4. **The Truth of the Path That Frees of Dukkha** ("The Prescription"): Following the eightfold path eliminates Dukkha caused by rebirth and the five aggregates. (*"Magga / Mārga"*)

The Four Noble Truths focus on the word **Dukkha** *(Pāli)* / **Duḥkha** *(Sanskrit)*. This word is sometimes loosely translated as "suffering" by Westerners but is a complex term that has multiple meanings such as unsatisfactoriness, incapability of satisfying, stress, or something not quite right.

- Dukkha refers to the unsatisfactory nature of our current "existence" due to two things: **rebirth** and the clinging to the **five aggregates**. These may be confusing to beginners and Westerners, and we will go more in-depth about them later in this book. However, they are important to Dukkha.

- **Rebirth** refers to the continual cycle of birth and death (arising and ceasing). When one dies, there is no permanent, unchanging, independent "self" or "soul" that continues on. Instead, your karma (actions) and a stream of consciousness give rise to the next existence in a "realm" of rebirth. Every new existence that arises and we cling to *is* Dukkha.

- Each existence, such as a human, consists of 'building blocks' known as the **Five Aggregates**. When arisen in this new and temporary and ever-changing form, the Five Aggregates work seamlessly together as something called "**Nāmarūpa**" which gives the *illusion* of a permanent, unchanging, and independent "self". Because this is not 'reality', but we believe it is, we cling to the belief in it and create actions (karma) that result in us remaining trapped in the cycle of rebirth. The Buddha said: *"In brief, the five aggregates subject to clinging are suffering."*

- Buddhists see the cycle of **rebirth** as something that is **not** wanted because it gives rise to **new existences** (Five Aggregates/Namarupa) which *is* **Dukkha**. "Life" itself isn't Dukkha, instead the cycle of rebirth where new forms constantly come in and out of existence, and the ignorance of that fact, allows Dukkha to exist.

- A Buddhist's **mission** is to clear away the confusion about "self" (**awakening**) so they can reside in their true state of **Nirvāṇa** where they have "blown out" the Three Fires of greed, anger, and delusion, which allows them to no longer cling and crave to the idea of "self", sensual objects, and creating actions (**Karma**) based upon it, which kept them trapped like a prisoner in rebirth.

5 – What is the Noble Eightfold Path?

The fourth Noble Truth in Buddhism is regarding the path to liberation, known as the **Noble Eightfold Path**. The eight parts are grouped into three categories practiced as the "**Threefold Training**".

It helps us overcome this 'affliction' or 'sickness' of "Dukkha" through the cultivation of specific disciplines:

1. Understand the truth about suffering ("**wisdom**") through Right **Understanding** and **Thoughts**.

2. Create the conditions to transcend suffering ("**conduct**" or "**morality**") through Right **Speech**, **Livelihood**, and **Action**.

3. Keep on the path towards awakening ("**discipline**" or "**meditation**") through Right **Effort**, **Mindfulness**, and **Concentration**.

Following the Noble Eightfold Path is the "prescription" the Buddha wrote so all sentient so we can heal our sickness ("Dukkha") caused by our delusions, desires, and attachments. This path is known as the "Middle Way", which means to not go to extremes when striving to realize enlightenment and Nirvāṇa.

The Noble Eightfold Path allows one to live their lives in perfect balance with the teachings, which in turn allow one to become awakened, realize enlightenment, not be trapped by Karma, live in their natural state of Nirvāṇa, which allows us to transcend the cycle of birth and death (rebirth).

1. **Right View:** The ability to have the right concepts and right ideas that lead away from delusion and wrong views.

2. **Right Thought:** Keeping thoughts in accord with the Buddha's Dharma. This is the "speech of your mind", therefore you want to ensure your thoughts align with Right View.

3. **Right Speech:** Ensuring your "verbal" Karma consists of words of truth, compassion, praise, and altruism.

4. **Right Action:** Ensuring your "bodily" Karma consists of not killing, not stealing, and not engaging in sexual misconduct.

5. **Right Livelihood:** Having the right occupation in life that does not harm others and ourselves.

6. **Right Effort:** Diligence in preventing unwholesome states that have yet to arise, ending unwholesome states that have arisen, and strengthening wholesome states.

7. **Right Mindfulness:** True contemplation where the mind is pure, aware, and does not give rise to unwholesome thoughts.

8. **Right Concentration:** Using samādhi (meditative concentration) to focus the mind and settle the distracted body to develop insight into the Buddha's truth (Pāli: vipassanā / Sanskrit: vipaśyanā).

Mahāyāna Buddhism places emphasis on cultivating the **Six Perfections (Pāramitās)** which are the **qualities of an enlightened being** (which correlate to the Eightfold Path). The Six Perfections[3] are *Giving*, *Morality*, *Patience*, *Diligence*, *Meditation*, and *Prajñā-Wisdom*.

For Mahāyānists, the development of these perfections, along with the Bodhisattva Vow and cultivation of Bodhicitta (enlightened mind), constitutes the disciplined "path" of a Bodhisattva that is working their way towards Buddhahood. Eventually becoming a Buddha is the ultimate goal for all Mahāyānists.

---

[3] Theravāda Buddhism has Ten Perfections (Pāramīs) which are *Giving*, *Virtue*, *Renunciation*, *Wisdom*, *Effort*, *Patience*, *Truthfulness*, *Determination*, *Loving-Kindness*, and *Equanimity*.

6 – What is Dependent Origination?

The truth the Buddha awakened to was that of **Dependent Origination** or **Conditionality** (*Sanskrit: Pratītyasamutpāda / Pāli: Paṭiccasamuppāda*). This is the teaching that is fundamental to all aspects of his teachings and mission. Dukkha, rebirth, karma, etc., all stem from this realization.

- Dependent Origination is the teaching that **all phenomena** (which include sentient beings such as you) **exist** and are **sustained** due to "**causes and conditions.**"

- It teaches we **do not** have a "self" that is **permanent, unchanging,** or "exists" **separately** from others. In other words, your "self" is **interdependent** upon and **conditioned** by other things.

- When causes and conditions no longer support the existence of phenomena, it **ceases** in that current form.

- There are **twelve links,** called Nidānas, that describe the entire process of Dependent Origination covering birth, death, and rebecoming.

To **explain** this concept at a basic level, we can use a Lotus flower:

- When the **right** causes and conditions arise (such as the soil, water, sun, nutrients) the flower starts to **grow** and eventually **blooms.**

- The flower, however, will **cease** in that form **eventually.**

- It was **never** something **permanent, unchanging,** or **independent** of other things to **exist.**

Why is Dependent Origination **important**?

- All <u>unenlightened</u> sentient beings have **ignorance** of the **truth** of Dependent Origination.

- This leads us down the road of **fueling** the **Three Poisons/Fires** of **greed**, **anger**, and **delusion** with our **attachments** to "**self**," the **karmic actions** that we create, and being trapped in an endless cycle of **rebirth** bound in saṃsāra – which *is* **Dukkha**.

- To **understand** *and* **end** Dukkha, we must fundamentally understand Dependent Origination to **free** ourselves.

- Unfortunately, we often **do not provide** the conditions to water or nourish the "seed" of enlightenment, so it never blooms.

- Fortunately, the Buddha **provides the teachings and practice** so that we can understand Dependent Origination and break down the belief in a permanent, unchanging, independent self.

Links of Dependent Origination (Nidānas)	Process / Result
Jarāmaraṇa : The impermanence of all conditioned bodies due to aging (present), decay, and death (future) of the body.	*Impermanence of life (Dukkha)*
Jāti: The birth or rebecoming of a phenomenon (Five Aggregates).	
Bhava: Coming into existence of the imaginary "self" and "world".	*The imaginary "self" and personalized "body" becomes the "self" in the "world"*
Upādāna The clinging to sensuality, views, vows, and the illusionary idea of "self".	
Taṇhā (Tṛṣṇā): The craving for sounds, smells, tastes, tactile sensations, ideas, sensuality, form, and formlessness.	
Vedanā: The feelings or sensations of vision, hearing, olfactory, gustatory, tactile, and intellectual sensation with your consciousness. Experienced as pleasant, unpleasant, and/or neutral feelings.	*Cognitive Process (Mana)*
Phassa (Sparśa): Contact with (sense impression) the sense object and consciousness.	
Saḷāyatana (ṣaḍāyatana): The experience of the six sense bases of the eye, ear, nose, tongue, body, and mind.	
Nāmarūpa: "Name and Form" which is the mental and physical components of a person working together seamlessly due to perception).	
Viññāṇa (Vijñāna): The sense consciousness of the eye, ear, nose, tongue, body, and mind.	*Process of Perception (includes Nāmarūpa)*
Saṅkhāra (Saṃskāra): Mental formations of the sensory entities we have visualized.	
Avijjā (Avidyā): Ignorance of the truth of Dukkha.	

7 – What is Karma?

When it comes to the concept and word "Karma" ("Kamma" in Pāli), you are likely to hear many explanations and definitions as to what it means. To make things confusing, the word has become part of the vocabulary in society and used in ways that do not reflect the Buddhist meaning.

The **Buddhist focus on Karma** is about:

- **Stopping** or **reducing** the amount of **unwholesome** karma we generate because it prevents us from reaching enlightenment, which keeps us in the cycle of birth and death.

- **Generating** more **wholesome** karma because it is skillful and helps us progress on the path towards enlightenment, which will eventually lead us out of the cycle of birth and death. While wholesome karma is important for creating the conditions for liberation, it is not sufficient alone.

- **Stop** creating "**any**" karma so we can **end our cycle of rebirth**. Enlightened beings generate "karma without outflows," and thus rebirth ends for them.

You **make** [wholesome or unwholesome] **karma** three ways:

- Your **Actions**

- Your **Thoughts**

- Your **Words**

By understanding these three things create either wholesome or unwholesome karma, you can work to **transform** them:

- Wholesome karmic actions are based upon **generosity**, **compassion**, **kindness**, **sympathy**, **mindfulness**, or **wisdom**.

- Unwholesome karmic actions are based upon the Three Poisons/Fires of **greed**, **hatred**, and **delusion**.

There are different types of karmic results:

1. **Negative Karma:** Actions that only produce negative karmic effects.

2. **Positive Karma:** Actions that only produce positive karmic effects.

3. **Both Negative and Positive Karma:** Actions that produce some negative, and some positive, karmic effects.

4. **Neither Negative nor Positive Karma:** Also known as "karma without outflows" is the type of karma of enlightened beings (such as the Buddha or one of his enlightened disciples).

5. **Neutral Karma:** When you committed a transgression that was not intentional or volitional.

The fundamental nature of Karma is that it **does not go away**. It is like a "seed" waiting for the **right conditions to bloom**. Right now, you have Karmic "seeds" within you since the time of your birth. This is because Karma **casually links all prior and future existences**.

While you cannot get rid of any "unwholesome" Karmic seeds, Buddhists focus on **generating good merit** which *is* wholesome Karma. Like salt in a glass of water, you can't remove the salt, but you can dilute it with more clean water.

8 – What is Not-Self?

A fundamental concept of Buddhism is that we do <u>not</u> have a **permanent, unchanging,** and **independent** "self" or "soul" (**Ātman**). Instead, we are a **temporary** grouping of things that create the **illusion** of "self" that we believe is permanent and unchanging. *This belief and attachment to "self" is the cause of Dukkha and Rebirth.*

To help remove this belief, and lead one away from Dukkha and Rebirth, the Buddha taught we do not have a permanent, unchanging, and independent self, which leads to *non-attachment* to that *idea* of self. This teaching is called **Anattā** (*Pāli*) or **Anātman** (*Sanskrit*) in Buddhism.

- Because we believe in this type of "permanent and unchanging self," we create **actions** (**Karma**) based on the **three poisons/fires** of greed, anger, and delusion, that keep us **trapped** in an endless cycle of **rebirth** (*Saṃsāra*) which is **unsatisfactory** (**dukkha**).

- One is "born" (arises) due to five components coming together called the "**Five Aggregates**" or "**Five Skandhas**" of <u>form</u>, <u>sensation</u>, <u>perception</u>, <u>mental formations</u>, and <u>consciousness</u>.

- The **Five Aggregates** – "you" – are a temporary condition that gives the **false impression** of a permanent, independent, and unchanging "self" due to all these components working very seamlessly together. This process creates the illusionary belief that we have something that is a permanent and unchanging "self" called "**Nāmarūpa**" ("name" and "form").

- Nāmarūpa works through our **sense organs** interacting with **sense objects**, and with the **mental formations** that arise, we *believe* what we **think, see, hear, feel,** etc., is "**real**." But that belief is **conditioned** by us and is **not** revealing the **true nature** of things.

The **Six Sense Organs** and **Six Corresponding Objects** are:

Organs	Objects
Eye	Visible Form
Ear	Sound
Nose	Odor
Tongue	Taste
Body	Tangible Feeling
Mind	Thoughts and Ideas

- Due to the belief that a permanent and unchanging "self" exists due to the Five Aggregates and Nāmarūpa, we **create fuel (attachments)** to support that belief. This is the source of **Dukkha**.

- The **Three Fires** of greed, anger, and delusion are fueled by your belief in self, and we then create intentional actions **(Karma)** *with* **outflows**. **Outflows** are like a ball and chain that keep you **trapped** in the cycle of rebirth. This cycle of rebirth is a beginningless and endless cycle of arising, ceasing, and rebecoming which is unsatisfactory (dukkha) which Buddhists strive to end.

9 – What is Rebirth?

A common **misconception** is that Buddhism believes in "**reincarnation**" where a permanent and unchanging "self" or "soul" transmigrates to a new body or existence. The Buddha firmly **rejected** this.

In Buddhism, the focus on "karma," and generating wholesome karma, is related to **rebirth**. The reason Buddhists want to achieve enlightenment and realize Nirvāṇa is to **stop** creating the types of **karma** that keep them trapped so they can end the cycle of birth and death known as *Saṃsāra*.

- The cycle of **rebirth** (*saṃsāra*), and thus our current existence, is **unsatisfactory** (**Dukkha**) due to the arising of this "self" (Five Aggregates) and the actions (Karma) we take. The Buddha taught us that this human realm in the cycle of rebirth is our best path to freedom because it allows us to become enlightened to the causes of Dukkha and rebirth and end it by residing within Nirvāṇa. Nirvāṇa allows us to only create Karma *without* outflows and thus ending rebirth (parinirvāṇa).

- For the unenlightened, Karma <u>with</u> outflows "**binds**" them in the cycle of rebirth – where they cling and grasp to things that feed their belief in a "self" that is permanent, unchanging, and independent. That karma, and other factors, determine what "realm" that karma is reborn in. But it is always a **temporary** existence in any realm (see page 57 for the different realms).

- One is "born" or "arises" in a new and temporary existence (such as a human being) due to causes and conditions (**Dependent Origination**) and the casual connection of **karma** between one life to the next. Karma is one of the four conditions[4] required for a new life to exist and the catalyst for rebirth.

---

[4] The other conditions are food, sense organs contact with sense objects, and consciousness.

- A **simile** of this cycle of birth and death is with a candle. The flame of a candle casually lights the wick of another candle. The two candles are not the same, and the flame (which is "karma" in this example) is what continues to the new existence (the "new" candle). When one realizes their true state of Nirvāṇa, they **blow out** that flame of Karma with outflows, so it does not keep them in *Saṃsāra*. When one who is fully enlightened passes away, they are freed from *Saṃsāra*.

- In <u>Mahāyāna</u> Buddhism, rebirth takes on a slightly different meaning for **fully enlightened beings** such as a **Buddha**, known as **dharmadhātu**. This dharmadhātu is the enlightened being's mindstream that is of pure essence and free of all attachments. Upon parinirvāṇa (final Nirvāṇa or death of the body/five aggregates), their mindstream is not only liberated from Saṃsāra but also the *illusionary* nature of both Saṃsāra and Nirvāṇa.

- Mahāyānists teach that a Buddha has "three bodies" known as **Dharmakāya**. Even though they do not arise in a new physical existence[5] after parinirvāṇa, they **exist in an expansive state** (a Buddha's *Reward Body*) where they may be realized during deep meditative states or by other means (for example, Amitabha Buddha's Western Pure Land is due to his *Reward Body*). Shakyamuni Buddha continues to have both a *Reward Body* <u>and</u> *Dharma Body*. A Dharma Body is essentially pure <u>truth</u> (Dharma) and <u>awakening</u> itself, which is the goal of all Buddhists.

---

[5] Shakyamuni Buddha had a Pure Land around him on this earth due to his *Reward Body*, but also had a *Manifested Body* that allowed ordinary beings to see and interact with him as a form of skillful means towards their awakening.

10 – What is Nirvāṇa?

Nirvāṇa (**Nibanna** in Pāli) is simply the end of all suffering (Dukkha). It has often been translated as meaning to "blow out" (or "extinguish"), so it can be confused with the term "extinction".

Thankfully, it has nothing to do with extinction. Nirvāṇa is the **blowing out of unwholesome things** (which are known as the "Three Fires") that cause suffering and dissatisfaction ("Dukkha") in our lives, and the creation of unwholesome actions ("Karma") that keep us trapped in the cycle of rebirth known as Saṃsāra. Saṃsāra *is* Dukkha, and Nirvāṇa *is* the **solution** to it.

- In the Buddhist world, unenlightened beings are **engulfed** in the **three fires** of **greed**, **anger**, and **ignorance** that are the root cause of **Dukkha** and **unskillful actions**.

- Because these "fires" are "**conditioned**", they can be **put out**. What remains after the fires are blown out, is **Nirvāṇa**. Nirvāṇa is the Buddha's Third Truth and your natural, or "true", state.

- An example of Nirvāṇa is the **embers of a fire that has been put out**. The fire is nice, we think, but it can also cause much destruction…which is why we often have it "safely" contained in an earthen, stone, steel, or metal structure. If we get too close, we could get burned, breathe in the smoke, or if the flames reach something flammable, it can ignite them. After the fire goes out, the embers are still quite hot or warm, but of course not as hot as the *flames* were! Those who have "blown out" the Three Fires are still very aware of them, and some "residual" heat exists. However, after some time, the embers are "cool". While it may sound scary to "blow out" these fires, the result is **cool and refreshing**: **Nirvāṇa**.

- While the **Five Aggregates** of their current existence remains, there is no longer "fuel" being poured on the Three Fires, and therefore no actions (karma) that bind them in rebirth.

- For a fully enlightened being, Nirvāṇa takes on another meaning when their physical body dies known as **parinirvāṇa** or **final Nirvāṇa**. Because they are no longer generating karma with outflows, they are **no longer bound to the cycle of rebirth** (*Saṃsāra*). At parinirvāṇa, they are no longer forced to "arise" in a new existence since they have eliminated the "conditions" that had been creating it.

- There is also the concept of **Non-Abiding Nirvāṇa** (Apradiṣṭhita Nirvāṇa) which is not "fixed", "stationary", or where you "dwell" in any single state of mind or position (i.e., Nirvāṇa or Saṃsāra). Non-Abiding Nirvāṇa is the perfect state of Buddhahood.

  o In <u>Theravāda</u>, there is only one type of Nirvāṇa which is firm in the Arhat's mind as the "other shore" of Nirvāṇa.

  o In <u>Mahāyāna</u>, the "static" concepts/labels of Nirvāṇa and Saṃsāra break down completely. One who realizes Non-Abiding Nirvāṇa is not "attached to" or "abides in" either. They are no longer caught in the cycle of rebirth (Saṃsāra) or limited to staying on the "other shore" (Nirvāṇa). Like a ferryman, they can come and go into the illusionary and conditioned world of "Saṃsāra" aiding others towards awakening.

How to Meditate

Sitting Meditation

Sitting meditation is a popular meditative practice. These basic steps can get you started:

1. Sit with your back straight.
2. Observe if there is any tension in the body and relax.
3. As your body relaxes, the attention will automatically go to the breath.
4. Observe the nature of the breath; is it long or short; obstructed or not?
5. Observe how you feel in the body as you breathe in.
6. As you keep doing this, the body begins to relax[6].
7. Then you begin to experience the comfortable feeling of relaxation.
8. Then you begin to experience satisfaction.
9. Focus your attention on the experience of satisfaction and comfort.
10. Observe any thoughts that arise in the mind
11. Observe the mood of the mind
12. Maintain attention on the breath and tranquility that arises from it.
13. Remain in this state of tranquil observation of the body and mind as long as possible.

Contemplative Meditations

Within all Buddhist traditions, there is another form of meditation which is called Anussati in Pali meaning to contemplate or reflect. Contemplative meditation serves the purpose of focusing and calming the mind. Contemplative meditations can help to increase confidence in the Buddha, Dharma, and Sangha.

Within the Theravāda tradition loving-kindness (metta) meditation is one of the more popular contemplative meditations. But you can also find meditations on a single word such as Budho, which is a popular contemplation in Thailand.

---

[6] Watch a video by Sanathavihari Bhikkhu on a body scan meditation: https://www.youtube.com/watch?v=8FDJrdfRaPU

Within the Mahāyāna tradition, you can find meditation such as Nāmó Āmítuófó of the Pure land school, Om mani padme hūm in the Tibetan school, and Nam Myōhō Renge Kyō in the Nichiren school.

These meditations are designed in part to help the practitioner embody the noble qualities of the Dharma. It is a skillful practice when we find it difficult to just focus on the breath or body due to our busy minds. We can use these contemplative practices to feed that busy mind something *wholesome* to ruminate on.

Loving-Kindness Meditation

In this practice, we generate goodwill towards all beings. Starting with oneself and gradually expanding it to include all beings. Just like in other meditation find a quiet and safe place to practice, sit comfortably with a straight back and close your eyes or gaze slightly downward away from any distraction. In the following practice please try to spend a few moments in every one of the steps:

1. *May I be well and happy*
2. *May all beings to the north of me be well and happy*
3. *May all beings to the west of me be well and happy*
4. *May all beings to the south of me be well and happy*
5. *May all beings to the east of me be well and happy*
6. *May all beings to the nadir (under) of me be well and happy*
7. *May all beings to the zenith (over) of me be well and happy*

How to Study the Buddhist Teachings

Personal Advice from Venerable Sanathavihari Bhikkhu

There are numerous ways that we can study the teachings of the Buddha. The first and foremost would be *living* the teachings in our everyday lives. However, to do this first we need some conceptual understanding of the teachings.

Many people ask me if they should read books of great contemporary teachers such as the Dalai Lama, Thich Nhat Hanh, Bhikkhu Bodhi, and many more. Or, if they should drive straight into the Sutta/Sutras. I think both are lovely options and depending on one's learning style either/or might be perfect for you.

Having said all of this I would like to propose another method, it is an ancient method and one that is still practiced to this day throughout the Buddhist world, which is *recitation*.

From the time of the Buddha to present day, followers of the Buddha have been chanting the teachings of the Buddha not only as a form of contemplative prayer or devotional meditation but as a way of comprehending the teachings. In fact, it was the Sammasam Buddha Gotama himself that taught in the form of recitation, and that is the way we have been transmitted the precious teachings up until this day.

Now I am not saying you must recite an entire liturgy or that you have a daily chanting routine. What I am suggesting is to find a teaching (sutra) that appeals to you such as the Heart Sutra or Metta Sutta and chant it in English or its traditional language of transmission.

There is a unique power that comes from chanting the teachings. Instead of one just trying to memorize or at minimum get the gist of the teachings, the teachings instead begin to resonate with oneself. Like that song that you feel in love with while you were in high school and can still recite to this day which still brings some visceral experience just as if you were back there again. This is what I like to call an experiential approach to studying the teachings of the Buddha.

Although having said all this I do believe that for many of us, including my past self, if we are completely new to Buddhism an introduction to Buddhism book can be a great way to start. Any book from *Buddhism for Dummies* to Bhikkhu Bodhi's *The Noble Eightfold Path* to the Dalai Lama's *The Joy of Living and Dying in Peace* (the book that started me in Buddhism).

Whichever root you take I would like to invite you to attempt to incorporate the teachings to whatever degree you can into your daily life and to make a ritual of sort of the learning process, we are creatures of habit, and doing is the best way to learn instead of trying to memorize.

How to Practice Buddhism in Everyday Life

"Bhikkhus, there are these three grounds for making merit. What three? The ground for making merit consisting in giving, the ground for making merit consisting in virtue, and the ground for making merit consisting in mind-development. These are the three." ~ The Buddha

---

How Buddhists practice is as varied as the many different traditions. However, the focus on cultivating *merit* is the **primary practice** of both laypersons *and* monastics.

Merit is the result of **good deeds**, **acts**, or **thoughts** in accord with the Buddhist teachings. It creates the right wholesome conditions for us to progress on the path towards enlightenment, realize Nirvana, and end the cycle of rebirth.

The Buddha realized that not everyone wanted to, or could, become a monastic (monk or nun), but they still needed a path they could follow in daily life. Through generating merit, **laypersons can create wholesome changes** within themselves and provide for future conditions that are beneficial on the path towards enlightenment. Even the Buddha in his prior lives was generating and cultivating merit that eventually cumulated in the right conditions for his final birth where he was able to become a Buddha.

So, how do you generate merit? Three main ways help us stop the Three Poisons/Fires of greed, anger, and delusion, which are the root cause of suffering Dukkha), unwholesome karmic actions, and rebirth:

1. **Giving (Dāna):** The first step and primary practice for any Buddhist to help stop the Three Poisons/Fires of greed, anger, and delusion. This practice alone was praised by the Buddha as one of the most important. While giving can be done in many ways, the Sangha (monastic community) is seen as the most meritorious field of merit to give to. In turn, monastics generate merit by teaching us, the laypersons, how to understand and practice the Dharma.

2. **Morality (Sīla):** To live a balanced life according to Buddhist ethics. One can do this through aspiring to follow the Five Precepts, or even by taking on additional precepts (which is why there are certain days and short-term retreats for this purpose).

3. **Mental Development (Bhāvanā):** The purification of the mind of the Three Poisons requires effort and determination. With Bhāvanā, you are not limited to sitting meditation alone. You can partake in chanting, reading, and reciting scripture, invoking the name of a Buddha, attending Dharma talks and services, venerating Buddhas and Bodhisattvas, mindfulness, etc.

These three elements work together: Without Sīla, our ability to truly develop the mind (Bhavana) is hindered. And without Dāna, we are unable to develop Sīla.

While it may seem like you are depositing "merit coins in the bank," there is another part to this practice: the ***transferring of merit***. This is where one does not "keep" the merit they just created but instead dedicates that merit (such as after a daily practice) to family members, those who are facing challenging times, or even to all sentient beings.

Monastics also do this by transferring merit to laypersons in the congregation that was generated during a Dharma service or other activity.

When transferring merit, it is done with a mind that is giving out of **compassion, generosity**, and **loving-kindness** which are fundamental Buddhist qualities.

When we transfer merit, we are also helping to transform and **purify our mind** by ridding it of ego, selfishness, greed, clinging, and craving that hinders us on the path.

How to Visit a Buddhist Temple

If you are fortunate to have a Buddhist temple (or several) in your town, you are likely curious how to "visit" a temple, and what you will experience.

There are numerous Buddhist traditions that all have a range of styles, designs, and etiquette as it relates to their temples. In Western countries, you are typically encountering temples that have cultural ties to the tradition and country they come from. The monastics and laypersons who go to the temple are coming from the same country, and therefore will meet their spiritual and cultural needs of them, typically in their native language.

While all of this can be a bit shocking to someone who is *not* from that culture, or even Buddhism in general, it is **nothing to be apprehensive about**. The following are suggestions on how to visit a Buddhist temple, and how to join the congregation.

1. **Use the internet** to see if they have a website that may provide some guidance on visiting the temple. Some larger temples are visited by tourists and visitors, while smaller ones may not.

2. **Contact the temple** about your intentions, and their recommendations. Typically, layperson volunteers help to manage temple websites (in addition to monastics) and may speak English. Ask if you can visit, etiquette to follow, and if they can have someone greet you. This way, you can be guided on your first visit.

3. During your visit, **ask about the tradition of Buddhism they practice** (you may also be told the "lineage," which refers to the line of succession that goes back to the Buddha), what laypersons do at the temple, and how you can start attending and learning. While it is fine to have questions to better understand, be respectful and do not negatively or dismissingly question their beliefs.

4. **Greeting** other laypersons, and especially monastics is usually done with **hands joined together and placed at the center of the chest** (sometimes with a bow). This is a gesture of respect and kindness. However, every tradition has diverse ways this

31

may be done so it is best to ask if you are already talking with someone.

5.   Depending on the temple and layout, you *might* need to **take off your shoes** which is common in many Asian cultures. However, one thing you should do is always **dress appropriately** as this is a religious site. This means no revealing clothing, taking off hats and sunglasses, etc. Also, as a general rule do not point, take pictures, touch things, eat food or drink, etc.

6.   Larger temples may have different "**rooms,**" to include the **main shrine** area, whereas smaller temples may have it all combined in one large room. In the main shrine room, you will usually see a state of the Buddha, or Buddhas, depending on tradition. This room is **treated with respect**, and there is often bowing before the Buddha to show respect. This is a wonderful opportunity to ask how to bow/prostrate before the Buddha in the tradition you are visiting.

7.   While it is best to make your first visit when services are not occurring if you do go during a service ensure you are **quiet and respectful** as to not disturb the service.

Visiting a temple provides you not only the opportunity to gain an understanding of Buddhism but also understand another culture. Please remember to be respectful and take the time to decide if this is a temple and tradition you would like to join.

How to Become a Buddhist

"How do I become a Buddhist?" The simple answer is to take refuge in the <u>Triple Gem</u>:

"I take refuge in the Buddha;
I take refuge in the Dharma;
I take refuge in the Sangha."

When one takes refuge in these three things, you are "officially" a Buddhist. There is no need to be part of any tradition, temple, group, or even teacher (although belonging to one is both traditional and has advantages). Depending on the tradition or temple you join, there may be an official refuge ceremony.

- Taking refuge means you are placing your **trust, faith, effort,** and **devotion** in the Buddha as our teacher, his Dharma as the teachings towards liberation, and the Sangha as the monastic community that teaches laypersons. We are going to **"refuge"** with them as the only way we can become enlightened, realize Nirvana, rid ourselves of the Three Fires of greed, anger, and delusion, which allows us to escape the cycle of birth and death that has caused Dukkha.

- **Taking refuge is like finding an oasis in a barren desert.** We may stumble upon this oasis in the middle of a large desert, drink and refresh ourselves, and then leave it to walk aimlessly and endlessly in the desert. This desert is like the endless cycle of birth and death, the suffering (Dukkha) that results, and our ignorance of the truth of suffering. Or we can realize that while we may not fully understand everything the Buddha taught, we realize his Dharma is like a refreshing glass of water in that desert and we should continue to nourish ourselves.

- **One does not need to "become" a Buddhist right away.** It is quite common to be an "observer of Buddhism" as you are learning and practicing. During this time, you are exploring and learning about the religion, but do not yet have the urge or desire to devote yourself fully to it. That is OK. When you have made the decision that the Buddha's path calls to you, then you can take refuge.

What about becoming a monk or nun? Westerners may be drawn to the imagery of monastics and want to immediately jump on a plane and become one without having ever practiced in the religion.

- **To become a monastic is often a lengthy process.** There is a period where the temple wants to see that you are serious about this and is not just a whim or wanting to escape everyday life. After a period of review, one may become a novice monastic and be 'reviewed' for several years. After several years, they may then officially become a monastic. Some traditions even have a sort of 'Buddhist college' that potential monastics must attend for years. While there may sometimes be 'temporary ordination' as a monk, this is often culturally specific and for generating merit.

- **If becoming a monastic is something you want to do**, first fully invest yourself in the religion for at least a year. Talk with the monastics about your intent and next steps. There are also often opportunities for short-term retreats for laypersons, classes, and more.

- While wanting to become a monastic is a very wholesome and serious path, it is *not mandatory*. The half-billion Buddhists around the world are laypersons and lead full religious lives as Buddhists, support the monastic community, engage in numerous ceremonies, rituals, and other activities, and can practice the Threefold Training and uphold precepts as laypersons.

Appendix A: Buddhist Resources

We encourage you to continue exploring the religion with this curated list. Note: Links can change at any time, and were accurate at the time of publication. This list is not meant as an endorsement.

Books

- The Heart of the Buddha's Teachings *By Ven. Thich Nhat Hanh*
- What in Brief is Buddhism *By Ananda W.P. Guruge*
- In the Buddha's Words *By Bhikkhu Bodhi*
- Awakening of the Heart: Essential Buddhist Sutras and Commentaries *By Ven. Thich Nhat Hanh*
- The Noble Eightfold Path: Way to the End of Suffering *by Bhikkhu Bodhi*
- What the Buddha Taught *by Richard Gombrich*
- The Joy of Living and Dying in Peace *by His Holiness the Dalai Lama*
- More: *https://alanpeto.com/buddhism/top-buddhist-books/*

Websites

- Dhammatalks (English translations of scripture from the Pali Canon)
  - *https://www.dhammatalks.org/*
- BDK America (English translations of scripture from the Chinese Canon)
  - *https://bdkamerica.org/tripitaka-list/*
- Buddhism for Beginners on Tricycle
  - *https://tricycle.org/topic/buddhism-for-beginners/*
- Buddhanet (Collection of Buddhist resources, eBooks, and more)
  - *http://www.buddhanet.net/*
- Buddhanet World Buddhist Directory (Directory of temples & groups)
  - *http://www.buddhanet.info/wbd/*
- Learn Religions with Barbara O'Brien (Buddhism)
  - *https://www.learnreligions.com/buddhism-4684851*

Podcasts

Note: Most podcasts can be found on your favorite podcast services & apps.

- AudioDharma
  - *https://www.audiodharma.org*
- Thich Nhat Hanh Podcasts
  - *https://tnhaudio.org/*
- The Way Out is In
  - *https://plumvillage.org/podcasts/the-way-out-is-in/*
- Bodhi Light Tales with Venerable Miao Guang
  - *https://foguangpedia.org/bodhi-light-tales/*
- Ajahn Sona
  - *https://anchor.fm/ajahn-sona*
- DhammaTalks with Thanissaro Bhikkhu
  - *https://www.dhammatalks.org/mp3_collections_index.html*
- Learn Buddhism with Alan Peto
  - *https://alanpeto.com/podcast*

Videos

- For a list of videos and channels on YouTube:
  - *https://alanpeto.com/buddhism/top-buddhism-videos/*

Appendix B: Buddhist Scriptures

This list is intended to aid you with one of the most asked questions: **"What Buddhist scriptures should I start reading?"** Before we provide you a list of scriptures, here are some important notes:

- **First, don't rush into it!** Buddhist scriptures are not only numerous but can be extremely overwhelming, especially for those new to Buddhism. While it is fine to read scripture, it should be coupled with that of a Buddhist teacher. This is because many of these scriptures were meant for monastics or have concepts and meanings which can be easily misunderstood.

- **Should you be reading scripture?** Reading scriptures should not be your primary focus in Buddhism. Instead, you should seek guidance and commentary from Buddhist monastics/teachers who can effectively explain *what* the Buddhist teachings *mean* and *how* to practice them.

- **How to start learning:** If you do not have a Buddhist temple or teacher nearby, an option for you would be to attend a virtual session with a temple. They may have classes or are reading a book that provides context and commentary to explain these scriptures and Buddhist teachings in general. Refer to Appendix A for some suggestions.

- **What's important and What's not?** The Buddhist traditions have different views on what should be read, recited, or chanted as part of a layperson's practice. Therefore, the list in this appendix will provide you with a "general" recommended reading list. Again, you should be working with a Buddhist teacher/temple in guiding you with understanding scripture.

- **Sūtras and Suttas:** East-Asian and Central-Asian Buddhism (Mahāyāna) calls sermons of the Buddha **Sūtras** and South-Asian Buddhism (Theravāda) calls them **Suttas**. The Pāli Canon and Chinese Canon both have the same sermons of the Buddha, although there may be minor variations due to translation and language. There are also Mahāyāna Sūtras which do not exist in South-Asian Buddhism and only exist in East-Asian and Central-Asian Buddhism.

- **Pāli and Sanskrit:** The scriptural languages of ancient India were Pāli and Sanskrit. The Theravāda school wrote their scriptural canon in Pāli, while the dozens of other schools wrote them in Sanskrit. However, the Buddha did not speak either of these languages because the scriptures were not written down until centuries after his death. Buddhism was an orally recited tradition until their oral canons began to be written down.

- There are three **scriptural canons** of Buddhism: *South-Asian Buddhism* has the **Pāli Canon** (Sri Lanka, Thailand, Laos, Cambodia, Myanmar), *East-Asian Buddhism* has the **Chinese Canon** (China, Taiwan, Vietnam, Japan, Korea), and *Central-Asian Buddhism* has the **Tibetan Canon** (Tibet, Mongolia, Russia, Bhutan).

Essential sermons of the Buddha you can read (regardless of Buddhist tradition) are:

- **"Setting in Motion the Wheel of the Dhamma"** (Dhammacakkappavattana Sutta).

- **"The Fire Sermon"** (Ādittapariyāya Sutta)

- **"The Discourse of the Not-Self Characteristic"** (Anatta-lakkhana Sutta)

- **"The Eightfold Path"** (Vibhaṅgasutta Sutta)

Additional sermons that will help the new Buddhist with core teachings and concepts:

- **Sigalovada Sutta:** The Buddha provides instructions for laypersons.

- **Anapānasati Sutta:** This Sutta covers the basics of breath meditation.

- **Maha-Satipatthana Sutta:** This Sutta covers the basics of mindfulness.

38

- **Sabbasava Sutta:** <u>Overcoming external influences</u> that pollute the mind.

- **Ambalatthika-rahulovada Sutta:** Teaching on <u>Virtue</u>.

- **Samadhanga Sutta:** Teaching on <u>Concentration</u>.

- **Dhatu-vibhanga Sutta:** Teaching on <u>Wisdom</u>.

- **Karaniya Metta Suta:** The practice of <u>loving-kindness</u>.

East-Asian Buddhism (China, Taiwan, Vietnam, Korea, Japan) and **Central Asian Buddhism** (Tibet, Mongolia, etc.) are within the "**Mahāyāna**" branch of Buddhism and include additional scripture <u>not</u> found in **Theravāda**. However, they are made up of numerous different schools which hold certain scriptures as more foundational than others.

- Regardless, the sermons of the Buddha (which includes the list you saw above) can all be found in the Chinese Canon of East-Asian Buddhism.

- There are several Mahāyāna Sūtras that are important, and widely read and chanted, in Mahāyāna Buddhism. The Mahāyāna Sūtras are what makes the Chinese Canon a Mahāyāna Branch of Buddhism Canon.

- You will likely be using some, or all, of these Sūtras more than you would anything else in your practice. This is because, in the Mahāyāna tradition, these Sūtras can be said to contain the essence of all the Buddha's teachings or advanced teachings. They can also help a practitioner to use them almost as a meditative tool through study and insight to gain awakening.

The following are some of **the most important and widely recited Mahāyāna sūtras**:

- The most widely referred to sūtra in Mahāyāna (generally) would be the **Heart** sūtra.

- Some of the popular Mahāyāna Sūtras are the **Heart, Diamond**, and **Lotus** Sūtras.

- Some sutras that are influential with Chán/Zen include the Decent into Lanka (**Lankavatara**), **Lotus, Diamond**, and **Flower Garland** (Avatamsaka) Sūtras.

- Some of the sūtras that are foundational with Pure Land Buddhism are the **Amitabha** (Shorter and Longer) and **Meditation** sūtras.

The following are just a few of the many **Mahāyāna Sūtras** and a brief explanation of each:

- **Amitabha [Shorter] (Sukhāvatīvyūha Sūtra):** The blessings and virtues of Amitabha Buddha, his Pure Land (Sukhāvatī), and rebirth.

- **Amitabha [Longer] (Sukhāvatīvyūha Sūtra):** Explains cause and effect (Karma), and describes the Western Pure Land (Sukhāvatī).

- **Meditation (Amitāyurdhyāna Sūtra):** Meditations and visualization of Amitabha Buddha's Western Pure Land (Sukhāvatī). This is the third of the three sutras that make up the doctrinal basis of the Pure Land school (the other two are the shorter and longer Amitabha sutras).

- **Brahma Net (Brahmajāla Sūtra):** The Ten Major Precepts of Mahāyāna followers and 48 Minor Precepts for Bodhisattvas to follow on the path.

- **Diamond (Vajracchedikā Prajñāpāramitā Sūtra):** The Buddha teaches how to cut through afflictions, ignorance, delusion, or illusion through the perfection of insight and wisdom (Prajñāpāramitā). This Sūtra is about the emptiness of all phenomena, wisdom, perception, and non-attachment. It is considered an extremely important Sūtra by Chan Buddhists.

- **Flower Garland (Av̇ataṃsaka Sūtra):** Explains how reality appears to an enlightened being (such as a Bodhisattva). A compilation of teachings on topics such as the ten stages on the Bodhisattva path, phenomena (dharmas), meditation/mind only (Vijñaptimatra), and emptiness (sunyata). It is the second-longest sutra in the Mahāyāna (40 chapters). It is said to record the higher teaching of the Buddha to Bodhisattvas and other high spiritual beings. Also referred to as the Flower Ornament Sutra, Flower Adornment Sutra, or Gandavyuha Sutra.

- **Heart (Prajñāpāramitā Hṛdaya Sūtra):** Through the perfection of insight and wisdom (Prajñāpāramitā), the Bodhisattva can see the emptiness (sunyata) of all phenomena (dharmas) known through (and as) the Five Aggregates. This is a Sūtra about wisdom (prajna). The Heart Sūtra is perhaps the most well known, and recited, among Buddhists, and is part of the Prajnaparamita group of sutras (the Diamond Sūtra is another one).

- **Jewel Heap (Mahāratnakūṭa Sūtra):** Collection of 49 texts of various lengths and topics such as wisdom (prajñā), illusion (māyā), skillful means (upāya), and the Western Pure Land (Sukhāvatī). This is one of the oldest sutras in the Vaipulya group of 49 independent sutras.

- **Decent into Lanka (Laṅkāvatāra Sūtra):** Scriptural basis of the Yogacara and Chán/Zen schools on the doctrines of the illusionary and empty nature of all phenomena as manifestations of the mind, that consciousness is our only true reality, culminating in the Tathāgatagarbha (i.e., Buddha-nature).

- **Ten Stages (Daśabhūmika Sūtra):** The Buddha describes the Ten Stages of Cultivation for Bodhisattvas on their path to full enlightenment and Buddhahood.

- **Vimalakīrti (Vimalakīrti Sūtra):** Teachings on the doctrines of non-duality and emptiness. It explains the illusionary nature of the world, the equality of women, and the enlightenment of laypersons.

41

- **Lotus (Saddharmapuṇḍarīka Sūtra):** Considered the sūtra of skillful means (upāya) providing a way for persons to readily achieve enlightenment, and stresses that every living being can achieve Buddhahood. As one of the smallest and most popular Mahāyāna Sūtras, it has become almost a central text in some schools such as Nichiren. Many Buddhists (schools and practitioners) consider the Lotus Sūtra the final teaching of the Buddha that contains all that is needed for enlightenment ("salvation") where all beings can become Buddhas. It is also considered the Sūtra of "upāya" or 'skillful/expedient means' meaning it provides a way for persons to achieve enlightenment more readily. This is also one of the oldest Mahāyāna Sūtras (believed to have been completed around 200 BCE). Theravāda monastic Bhikkhu Sujato believes it may even predate Mahāyāna as it was likely worked on over some time and the earliest form of it was before Mahāyāna.

Learn more about the Buddhist scriptures and canons:
https://alanpeto.com/buddhism/buddhist-scriptures

Appendix C: Buddhist Traditions

There are two major "branches" of the Buddhism tree in our modern world: **Theravāda** and **Mahāyāna** Buddhism.

More specifically, Buddhism is grouped geographically into South-Asian Buddhism (which only practices "Theravāda"), and East-Asian and Central-Asian Buddhism (predominantly practicing "Mahāyāna" since they include Mahāyāna scriptures) which have many different "schools".

- **As a layperson, there is no wrong "path" to take.** All schools, sects, and traditions of Buddhism believe in and follow the **core teachings** of the Buddha. This includes the Four Noble Truths, Noble Eightfold Path, the Buddha's Sermons (Sūtras), and teachings such as Rebirth, and Karma.

- The major difference is the **"path"** one takes: Theravāda (**Arhat** Path) and Mahāyāna (**Bodhisattva** Path). This is categorized as the **"Three Vehicles" (Yānas)**

  o Śrāvakayāna: Arhat/Arhant (Listeners/Disciples) - Achieves individual enlightenment & Nirvāṇa through the teachings of a Buddha (may rarely be called Sāvakabuddha). Only the Theravāda school follows this path.

  o Pratyekabuddhayāna: Solitary Buddhas - Discovers the Dharma but is unable to teach others (this is not a current path since we have teachings to follow).

  o Bodhisattvayāna: Bodhisattva Path - The path towards becoming a fully awakened Buddha to fulfill the aspiration to save all sentient beings. All the other Buddhist schools follow this path (Mahāyāna) which includes Zen (Ch'an, Thien, Seon), Pure Land, Tibetan, Nichiren, etc.

- The other major difference is different views on **"Buddhavacana"**, which is the **"Word of the Buddha"**. This refers to scripture that is in accord with the teachings of the Buddha leading towards enlightenment and Nirvāṇa.

  o Theravāda: The Pāli Canon contains the Buddhavacana for Theravāda. They do not accept the Mahāyāna sūtras as Buddhavacana.

  o Mahāyāna: A more progressive view that the Buddha's teachings, and his disciples, are Buddhavacana. This includes Buddhas, disciples of the Buddha, Rishi (enlightened persons), and Devas. Scripture is found in the Chinese Canon and Tibetan Canon.

- **Doctrinal Differences**

  o Buddha: Considered supermundane in Mahāyāna; Buddhas have a different realization than other enlightened persons. Theravāda says the same human body and realization as Arhats but have taken a longer path. Mahāyāna also has numerous Buddhas, Bodhisattvas, and "Buddha Fields" (Pure Lands) that one can have rebirth in to be under the guidance of a living Buddha.

  o Buddhanature: In Mahāyāna, all sentient beings have the innate capability to become a Buddha. In Theravāda, one can only become a Buddha [of an era] if predicted by a Buddha eons ago.

  o Bodhisattva: In Mahāyāna anyone can be on the Bodhisattva path either as unenlightened or at different stages of enlightenment. Theravāda says only for exceptional beings and as unenlightened.

Buddhist Schools

Based upon the two branches of Buddhism, there are several different "schools" that exist. These schools teach and practice their branch (and path) of Buddhism in a way that is unique to them while staying true to the heart of Buddhism as the Buddha taught it.

While **Theravāda** is the only school within it's branch, there are several country-specific variations of it. These variations (which contain "Nikāya" in their names) are mainly related to the Vinaya (monastic rules). In **Mahāyāna** there are numerous schools that all practice the Bodhisattva path, but in ways that are unique to them.

This list is not meant to be all encompassing and covers a select number of schools.

South-Asian Buddhism (Theravāda)

Also known as the "southern transmission", South-Asian Buddhism started largely with the patronage of King Ashoka who sponsored monastics to spread the Buddha's teachings to neighboring countries. Theravāda is the only branch, and school, of Buddhism that does not teach the Mahāyāna path or contain Mahāyāna scriptures.

The countries of **Sri Lanka**, **Thailand**, **Burma**, **Cambodia**, **Laos**, **Vietnam**, and **Bangladesh** practice Theravāda.

India contains two movements not related to Theravāda. The Dalit Buddhist movement (founded by B.R. Ambedkar) was a neo-Buddhist movement for the Dalits in India. Tibetan Buddhism can be found in India due to refugees that came from Tibet.

- **Burma** contains several traditions, however, the Vipassana Meditation movement has caught worldwide attention. It was created in Burma by the monk Ledi Sayadaw

- **Thailand** has Mahasati Meditation which is a form of mindfulness meditation that was created in Thailand by the monk Luangpor Teean Cittasubho that focuses on bodily movement and self-awareness. There is also the Thai Forest Tradition is where the monks follow the Buddha's attainment of enlightenment while he was in

45

the forest. This ascetic and disciplined tradition are most well known in the West due to Westerners who became monks and introduced the tradition to others.

East-Asian Buddhism (Mahāyāna)

Also known as the "northern transmission", East-Asian Buddhism started with **China** which was the first to receive scriptures, monks, and exchange of information from ancient India. Buddhism spread to **Vietnam, Korea**, and **Japan** often by Chinese Buddhist monks and dialog between countries. Mahāyāna can also be found in **Malaysia** and **Singapore** largely due to the migration of Chinese Buddhists.

Of interest is that there is a now-extinct school of Buddhism, *Yogācāra*, which lives on in the traditions that developed in East-Asian and Central-Asian Buddhism (Mahāyāna). Yogācāra delved into the nature of consciousness through meditative and yogic practices to include wisdom, morality, and concentration, and how it allows one to attain enlightenment. Traditions such as the meditation school (Zen / Ch'an) and others use elements of the Yogācāra school to practice and for the explanation and understanding of our world and mind.

There are largely two main schools: The **meditation** (dhyāna) school, which is called Ch'an in China, Zen in Japan, Thiền in Vietnam, and Seon in Korea, and the **Pure Land** school (which is perhaps the most widely practiced). There are also other traditions, such as the Nichiren school in Japan.

East-Asian Buddhism largely follows the Vinaya (monastic rules, ordination, and lineage) of the *Dharmaguptaka* school from ancient India.

- **Chinese Buddhism** today is largely defined by two dominant traditions: Ch'an (Chinese for dhyāna or "meditation") and Pure Land. However, the fluidity between temples and traditions means that both can often be found intermingled and practiced together. There is also the growing Humanistic Buddhism movement which is focused on practicing Buddhism in the human world, rather than focusing on after death.

- **Japanese Buddhism** features Buddhist schools that are structured differently than most of the Buddhist world. The Vinaya (monastic code) may be less emphasized with the schools meaning monastics can marry, eat meat,

46

and live a householder life. Laypersons may become "priests", which is not found elsewhere. And the schools are distinctly separated (such as Pure Land, Zen, and Nichiren) and do not intermingle, whereas you can find that occur without concern in countries such as China and Vietnam.

- **Vietnamese Buddhism** was largely shaped by China (and thus Mahāyāna) to include Thiền (Meditation "Ch'an"), Tịnh độ (Pure Land), and Thiên Thai (Tiantai). While Mahāyāna plays the central role in Vietnam (largely with Pure Land), the intermingling of Theravāda elements can be found.

- **Korean Buddhism** is largely of the Seon (mediation) school, but also includes elements found in Pure Land such as reciting the name of Amitābha Buddha. This dual approach is similar to what can be found in China and Vietnam but was developed to be specific to meet the interpretation of Korea. There are also modern Buddhist movements that focus on "Buddhism for the masses" known as Minjung Buddhism.

Central-Asian Buddhism (Mahāyāna)

Part of the "northern transmission" is Central-Asian Buddhism. This is practiced in the countries of **Tibet**, **Bhutan**, regions of the **Himalayas**, **Mongolia**, and **Russia** (**Siberia**). India can also be found to practice Central-Asian Buddhism due to refugees from Tibet.

While it developed independently of East-Asian Buddhism, it would eventually take some elements from the Chinese Buddhist Canon and follows the Bodhisattva Path (Mahāyāna) in their unique way. Some elements found practiced in Central-Asian Buddhism can be found in East-Asian Buddhism since both found inspiration and teachings from the many schools of ancient India.

Sometimes referred to as Vajrayāna Buddhism, it contains esoteric and yoga practices (among others) to attain Buddhahood in the fastest way possible. Because this method can be dangerous, only specific teachers called Lamas can teach students.

Several schools exist; however, most Westerners may be familiar with the Gelug school (Yellow Hat) since the 14th Dalai Lama is the leader of that tradition.

Appendix D: Buddhist Practice

All Buddhist practice is centered around the Buddha's **Eightfold Path**, which generates **wholesome merit** leading towards **awakening** and the mental state of **Nirvāṇa**, as explained by the Buddha. However, the different Buddhist traditions have their forms of practice. *This introduction will focus on the Eightfold Path as the foundational teaching.*

The Path is grouped into three distinct categories which form what is known as the "**Threefold Training**" in Buddhism. These three categories are interconnected and, when fully understood and practiced in one's life, form the right causes and conditions for awakening.

The **Threefold Training**, and groups of the Eightfold Path, are:

- **Wisdom**

    o *Training:* Cultivation of Wisdom

    o *Parts of the Eightfold Path:* Right Understanding and Right Thought.

- **Conduct (or Morality)**

    o *Training:* Cultivation of Morality

    o *Parts of the Eightfold Path:* Right Speech, Right Livelihood, and Right Action.

- **Discipline (or Meditation)**

    o *Training:* Meditative Concentration

    o *Parts of the Eightfold Path:* Right Effort, Right Mindfulness, and Right Concentration.

The formula to understanding why there are three categories, and parts of the practice, are as follows: *"**Meditation**" requires "**Morality**", and "**Wisdom**" requires "**Meditation**".*

If one does not have proper cultivation of morality, meditation will not bear the right fruits. If one only studies Buddhism intellectually without also focusing on settling the mind, they cannot gain true insight.

- Layperson Buddhists around the world practice this Threefold Training in **many ways** depending on the tradition they follow. However, the **cultivation of morality** and **generation of merit** are the most important things that many Buddhists practice in everyday life.

- They will then complement that practice by **attending ceremonies** and **services** at a Temple where they will **recite** scripture (sutra/sutta) or mantra, **invoke** the name of a Buddha, **listen** to Dharma talks by a monastic, and in **meditation** and/or **chanting**. Many will attend, at least once a year, short-term retreats or even a one-day Eight Precepts retreat where they will live a modified monastic life to recharge their faith.

- Each day you live your life, you will encounter the "Three Fires" (Three Poisons). The Three Fires are delusion & ignorance, greed & sensual attachment, and aversion & anger. Whenever you add fuel to these 'fires', you create the conditions for unwholesome Karma (volitional actions).

The Eightfold Path provides instructions for you to stop adding 'fuel to the fire'.

To learn how to practice Buddhism daily, refer to the next two pages. When you find a Buddhist tradition you wish to follow, please use their structure for a daily practice.

For instructions on how to practice Buddhism daily, refer to this article, video, and graphics: https://alanpeto.com/buddhism/daily-buddhist-practice/

Daily Buddhist Practice Quick Start

On these two pages, you will find an easy-to-follow list to aid with you starting a daily practice in a general format that is rooted in the Buddhist traditions.

1: Provide Offering(s)

- Flower
- Water
- Fruit
- Burn Incense
- Light a Candle

2: Prostrations

- Bow and/or prostrate three times in front of a statue or picture of The Buddha, Amitabha Buddha, a Buddhist teacher, etc.

3: Take Refuge in the Triple Gem

- "I take refuge in the Buddha,
- "I take refuge in the Dharma,
- "I take refuge in the Sangha"

4: Recite the Five Precepts

- "I will refrain from taking life,
- "I will refrain from stealing or taking what is not freely given,
- "I will refrain from sexual misconduct,
- "I will refrain from false speech, and
- "I will refrain from consuming intoxicants and illegal drugs."

5: Recite the Five Remembrances

- "I am subject to aging. There is no way to avoid aging.
- "I am subject to ill health. There is no way to avoid illness.
- "I am going to die. There is no way to avoid death.
- "Everyone and everything that I love will change, and I will be separated from them.
- "My only true possessions are my actions, and I cannot escape their consequences."

6: Recite, Chant, or Read Scripture (Sūtra)

- Refer to pages 25 and 37 for suggestions.

7: Meditate or Chant for 5-10 Minutes (or Longer)

- Straighten your spine & relax the muscles in your body.
- There are various meditative practices, however, counting the breath is a popular practice for beginners. Perform one count for the inhalation and another count for the exhalation. Count to ten and start over. If you forget your count, simply start over. As you quiet the mind, keep maintaining awareness of the breath.
- During your meditation, observe any thoughts arising in your mind and let them go.
- Chanting the Nianfo/Nembutsu (Refer to page 25)

8: Dedicate Merits of Practice

- "For all sentient beings, I dedicate the meritorious actions of this practice so they may be guided and liberated from delusion and suffering with the light of the Buddha's Dharma."

Appendix E: Buddhist Religion

There is often a question as to whether Buddhism is a "philosophy," "way of life," or a "religion." This can stem from Western concepts of religion (and experiences with it) that make us want to label something a "real religion," or not, based on a specific set of beliefs.

While Buddhism is a non-monotheistic religion of Indian origin, **it *is* as much a religion as others**.

The Oxford Dictionary has one definition of religion as a *"particular system of faith and worship"*, and Wikipedia has a general explanation of religion as a *"social-cultural system of designated behaviors and practices, morals, worldviews, texts, sanctified places, prophecies, ethics, or organizations, that relates humanity to supernatural, transcendental, or spiritual elements. However, there is no scholarly consensus over what precisely constitutes a religion."*

Based on the above, we can conclude that Buddhism is a complete religion with:

- A **central religious figure** which is the **Buddha**, and depending on the tradition, other Buddhas

- **Salvific teachings** / a **salvation message** that you can transform suffering and end wrong actions, which leads to the end of rebirth

- An **explanation of existence and life after death** which includes Saṃsāra, Nirvāṇa, Karma, Rebirth, etc.

- Dedicated **religious adherents** (Monks and Nuns)

- **Religious centers** (temples)

- **Rituals** include religious services, funeral services, chanting, meditation, pilgrimage, etc.

- **Ceremonies** (including the Triple Gem, Five Precepts, Bodhisattva Precepts, etc.)

- **Structure and methods of practicing** the religion by lay-followers

- **Faith** in the Buddha's teachings being true (even when we do not understand it all)

- **Cultural inclusion, holidays, beliefs**, etc. (might also be the national religion or a major religion)

- **Holy pilgrimage places** (with most ancient ones found in India and Nepal)

- **Heavenly and supernatural beings** such as gods, Bodhisattvas, demons, deities, etc.

- **Scripture** related to future Buddhas (i.e., prophecies)

- **Analysis and philosophy** of the scriptures, teachings, and religion (Abhidharma / Abhidhamma)

For 2,600 years, Buddhism has continued to develop based on the needs of its followers while staying true to the core teachings. The religion's commentary, analysis, practices, and rules, evolved even during the days of the Buddha, and continue to this day.

This growth is seen by some Westerners as an influence by cultural norms of the societies Buddhism spread to. But that is exactly what religion is. Religion is the "grease on the wheels" that helps complex Buddhist teachings be understood *and* practiced.

Even though you may not fully understand or even accept everything right away, any exposure and practice of Buddhism are wholesome. **Take it slow, and please be respectful.**

Our faith is not blind faith, but one where we look to the guidance of our teachers and the teachings as being true.

Along with our effort and determination to remove the ignorance in our mind and the resulting delusion, we can eventually understand the truth of the Buddhadharma[7] ourselves.

---

[7] Buddhadharma is the Buddha's teachings

Appendix F: Buddhist Ethics

When one thinks of the *behavior* of a "Buddhist," *ethics* immediately come to mind. For a moment, picture the Buddha, or even well-respected Buddhist monastics such as Thích Nhất Hạnh and The Dalai Lama. They demonstrate a "**demeanor**" or "**attitude**" we feel comfortable being around, it frees them of unjust criticism, their actions (karma) do not harm others, and they have harmony with all aspects of a life that is in balance with Buddhist teachings and thought. This is the result of *Buddhist ethics* or "*Śīla*."

"**Precepts**" are how Buddhists practice Buddhist ethics which align their life and practice with that of the Buddhist teachings. The Eightfold Path and the Perfections have "**Morality**" & "**Conduct**" within them which helps one demonstrate the Buddhist values of **compassion**, **generosity**, and **loving-kindness**.

Precepts are sometimes called "**rules**" by Westerners but should be looked at another way: **a practice that frees you**. Buddhists *willingly* aspire to take on and abide by the precepts because they *are* Buddhists and *want* to be freed from fueling the Three Fires of greed, anger, and delusion, the karmic actions that occur based on them, remaining trapped in the cycle of rebirth (due to karma), and endless rebirth - which is Dukkha. Precepts help us correctly walk the middle path in Buddhism that leads to liberation.

The Five Precepts

While the basic requirements for being a Buddhist is to take refuge in the Triple Gem (Buddha, Dharma, and Sangha), the Five Precepts are the next step to help transform their conduct. By following the Five Precepts, one does not create the conditions that harm or violate others through the volitional deeds of body, mind, and speech (karma). The Five Precepts are *foundational* in all traditions.

1. *To refrain from killing, harming, or violating others*
2. *To refrain from stealing or taking what is not yours*
3. *To refrain from sexual misconduct*
4. *To refrain from lying, gossip, or harsh speech*
5. *To refrain from consuming intoxicants or stimulants*

Bodhisattva Precepts

Mahāyāna Buddhists often aspire to take the Bodhisattva Precepts ("*bodhisattva-śīla*"). These demanding precepts align with the Bodhisattva vow where one aspires to liberate all sentient beings by being on the long path towards Buddhahood. The ten major Bodhisattva precepts are:

1. *Not to kill or encourage others to kill*
2. *Not to steal or encourage others to steal*
3. *Not to engage in licentious acts or encourage others to do so*
4. *Not to use false words and speech or encourage others to do so*
5. *Not to trade or sell alcoholic beverages or encourage others to do so*
6. *Not to broadcast the misdeeds or faults of the Buddhist assembly, nor encourage others to do so*
7. *Not to praise oneself and speak ill of others or encourage others to do so*
8. *Not to be stingy or encourage others to do so*
9. *Not to harbor anger or encourage others to be angry*
10. *Not to speak ill of the Buddha, the Dharma, or the Sangha or encourage others to do so*

Appendix G: Buddhist Cosmology

Buddhism has an extremely complex and detailed *cosmology* that is both **spatial** (different worlds or realms) and **temporal** (how the universe comes into being and is then dissolved). We can look at Buddhist cosmology in this way: they are teachings of **impermanence, dependent origination**, and **karma**, among other things.

A major component of Buddhism is **rebirth**. This is a foundational teaching that explains we are "suffering" due to our constant arising in forms (such as a human) in an endless cycle of rebirth (Saṃsāra). Buddhists actively practice (such as the generation of merit) for future existences to arise in the human realm (for reasons described below) with conditions that bring them closer to enlightenment.

These are **six literal realms of rebirth**. Buddhists aspire to always have their mind in the right 'realm,' and work towards having a good rebirth in the right realm in the future so they can continue on the path. *All* these realms are considered Dukkha, and the goal of Buddhists is to end rebirth in *all* of them.

1. **Devas or gods realm:** While many aspire to be reborn in this pleasure-filled realm due to wholesome karma, where existence can last for eons, it is still temporary.

2. **Human realm:** This is a *fortunate* realm because it is the only one that provides the right balance to understand the Dharma, practice it, attain Nirvana, and end Saṃsāra.

3. **Demigod realm:** An 'evil' realm where they often fight with those in the 'gods realm.'

4. **Animal realm:** A very 'hellish' realm due to acting upon 'impulse and instinct.'

5. **Hungry ghosts realm:** Suffering caused by a constant craving for attachments they cannot fulfill.

6. **Hell realm:** Those who have created evil karma enter this realm (violation of the Five Precepts).

An important component of all these realms is that existence in any of them is *impermanent*. When karma has been exhausted in a realm, one is reborn in another realm. The Buddha said that the Human realm was desirable because it has the right conditions for enlightenment. However, the human realm is also a very *rare* existence for rebirth, so one should use this opportunity to devote themselves to the path.

There are **three realms of existence** that are associated with the attainment of certain meditative states (Pali: **jhāna**, Sanskrit: **dhyana**). It consists of the <u>desire</u> realm (kāmadhātu) where one is bound by sensual desire and encompass the six realms described above, the <u>form</u> realm (rupadhātu) where one ascends through the five worlds within it, and finally the <u>formless</u> realm (Ārūpyadhātu) where those inhabitants have no shape or form and have attained higher levels of 'formless' meditative skills known as Arūpadhyānas. Even in the formless realm which *seems* desirable, one will eventually return to a lower state of existence when their merit or karma is exhausted.

There are also "**Pure Lands**" in Mahayana Buddhism where one can be reborn in to be under the guidance of a celestial Buddha to achieve enlightenment and become a Buddha. The most popular is Amitābha Buddha and his Western Pure Land known as *Sukhāvatī*.

You will often hear the word "**kalpa**" which is a unit of time (around 16 million years to hundreds of billions of years). It is recognized "we" have been trapped in Saṃsāra for countless kalpas and may be for more until we finally attain Nirvana. For Mahāyānists, it is understood that the Bodhisattva path towards Buddhahood will take many kalpas (in much the same way Shakyamuni Buddha did).

Appendix H: Buddhist Masters

Learning Buddhism is best done through monastics at the temple you will practice at. However, many will not have one close to them and strive to look for a Buddhist teacher. This list provides some popular contemporary Buddhist teachers who have books, videos, and other resources available.

- **Thích Nhất Hạnh:** (Mahāyāna) A Vietnamese Buddhist monk who became world-famous in the 1960s due to his opposition to the Vietnam war. He met with Dr. Martin Luther King, Jr., who would later nominate him for the Nobel Peace Prize. While his teachings focus on mindfulness, his teaching style was widely accessible to Westerners. You can find over 100 books written by him who is the founder of the international Plum Village community. *https://plumvillage.org/*

- **Hsing Yun:** (Mahāyāna) A Chinese Buddhist monk who established the worldwide Fo Guang Shan (FGS) Buddhist order based in Taiwan that focuses on Humanistic Buddhism (Buddhism that meets the needs of people and is integrated into all aspects of daily life). His numerous books explain Buddhism, Buddhist teachings, and the many Buddhist sūtras, especially those in Mahāyāna Buddhism. *https://hsingyun.org/*

- **Bhikkhu Bodhi:** (Theravāda) An American Buddhist monk who was ordained in Sri Lanka. He is the author of numerous Buddhist publications and books, including those that explain the Pāli Canon of Theravāda Buddhism. *https://bodhimonastery.org/ven-bhikkhu-bodhi.html*

- **Ajahn Chah:** (Theravāda) A Thai Buddhist monk who became influential due to founding two major monasteries of the Thai Forest Tradition. His teachings and monasteries were the first to bring Theravāda Buddhism to the West. *https://ajahnchah.org/*

- **Mahāsī Sayādaw:** (Theravāda) A Burmese Buddhist monk who is most famous for the development of what is now known as Vipassanā meditation. This brought a revival movement for laypersons in practicing meditation and grew popular in the West.
  https://en.wikipedia.org/wiki/Mahasi_Sayadaw

- **The 14ᵗʰ Dalai Lama:** (Mahāyāna) A Tibetan Buddhist monk and spiritual leader of the "Yellow Hat" school of Tibetan Buddhism. The name Dalai Lama is a title given to each manifestation of Avalokiteśvara Bodhisattva and is of political and religious significance. The current Dalai Lama is the 14ᵗʰ to hold the position and was born Tenzin Gyatso. In 1959, he fled Tibet and is a refugee in India. He is perhaps the most well-known Buddhist due to his decades of attention on the world stage, meeting with foreign dignitaries and celebrities. However, he is also a prolific writer who has written several popular books that explain Buddhist teachings and practice from the Tibetan Buddhist perspective.
  https://www.dalailama.com/

Glossary

- **Amitābha:** The Buddha of infinite light, commonly referred to as Amitābha or Amida. Amida has a Buddha 'Pure Land' in the 'West' where anyone can more easily achieve awakening. Pure Land Buddhists recite his name (through the 'Nembustu' – Japanese, 'Niànfó' – Chinese, 'Yeombul' – Korean, and 'Niệm Phật' – Vietnamese) as the primary part of their practice.

- **Arhat:** An enlightened individual who has freed themselves from the cycle of rebirth (Saṃsāra).

- **Avalokiteshvara:** A popular Bodhisattva that encompasses the compassion of all Buddhas. Also called Guanyin in China, and Kannon in Japan

- **Bhikkhu:** Bhikkhu (Pāli) or Bhikṣu (Sanskrit) is a mendicant and name for ordained male monks. Bhikkhunī (Pali) or Bhikṣuṇī (Sanskrit) is the term for ordained female nuns.

- **Bodhisattva:** An enlightened being who works to help all sentient beings, and not just themselves, to attain enlightenment and Buddhahood. They voluntarily remain in the cycle of rebirth (Saṃsāra) to help others.

- **Bodhidharma:** The patriarch of Zen/Chán Buddhism, who was a Buddhist monk that lived during the 5th or 6th century. He is credited with bringing the meditation school, known as Chán, to China. It eventually went to Japan as Zen, Korea as Seon, and Vietnam as Thiền.

- **Buddha:** Generally, is the title for one who is "awake" (awakened/enlightened). We use this single name to refer to the current Buddha of our era known as Gotama Buddha or Shakyamuni Buddha. However, the term "Buddha" is not restricted to Shakyamuni. In Mahayana Buddhism, all beings strive towards eventually becoming a Buddha, even if that takes eons. This is different than Shakyamuni Buddha, who is known as a 'Buddha of our era.' Each era has a single Buddha whose teachings we know and follow. Mahayana also has

61

other Buddhas, such as Amitābha, Medicine Buddha, etc. Both Mahayana and Theravada recognize the next Buddha of our era is known as Maitreya.

- **Buddha Nature:** The teaching that all sentient beings, like humans, have the natural ability to be able to realize enlightenment.

- **Buddhism:** Buddhism is a worldwide religion with over 350 million followers, based on the insight and teachings of the founder *Shakyamuni Buddha*. The Buddha's teachings allow us to be awakened to seeing our world as it is, free of delusion, greed, and hatred. This allows us to realize enlightenment and live in our natural state of Nirvāṇa, which liberates us from creating actions, typically unskillful and unwholesome, known as Karma. This ultimately allows us to transcend the endless cycle of birth and death, known as Saṃsāra, which was caused by our actions due to constant craving and attachment.

- **Chanting:** Chanting is a popular form of practice in most forms of Buddhist traditions. Typically, a teaching of the Buddha (called a Sūtra or Sutta) is recited or chanting the name of a Buddha. Chanting is similar to meditation because it allows a concentrated effort on an object, such as the Buddha and the Buddha's qualities, which aims to transform the mind of the practitioner towards awakening.

- **Dependent Origination:** A Buddhist concept explaining conditionality. All phenomena do not exist independently of other things, do not have a separate independent self, and are not permanent. All phenomena arise and fall, dependent on causes and conditions.

- **Dharma:** The teachings or sermons of the Buddha or one of his enlightened disciples. Also called the "Buddhadharma."

- **Dharmas:** "Dharmas" are phenomena and beings. It is not to be confused with the similarly worded 'Dharma,' which are the teachings or sermons of the Buddha.

- **Dukkha:** Called "Dukkha" in Pāli and "Duḥkha" in Sanskrit. Dukkha is a term that is sometimes translated as "Suffering" or "Unsatisfactoriness." Dukkha is a result of our attachments, specifically to the erroneous belief that we (and other things) have an unchanging, independent, and permanent 'self.' Our attachments to things create actions (Karma), which result in Dukkha, which is the "sickness" we face. This sickness, which creates Karma, results in rebirth. Attachments crave "fuel," which they find with the "Three Poisons/Fires" of Ignorance/Delusions, Greed/Desire, and Aversion/Hatred. These are essentially 'wrong views' which cause us to have cravings, which in turn cause us to be "attached" to Saṃsāra. Following the Noble Eightfold Path, which is likened to a "prescription" the Buddha wrote, all sentient beings like humans can heal our sickness ("Dukkha") caused by the three poisons.

- **Eightfold Path:** This core teaching of the Buddha describes the path towards awakening and enlightenment, which allows one to live in the state of Nirvāṇa.

- **Emptiness:** The concept of 'emptiness' is different in Mahāyāna Buddhism than it is in Theravāda Buddhism. Mahāyāna Buddhists believe that not only are human beings empty of an intrinsic self (such as a soul), but everything (all phenomena, which are called 'dharmas') is inherently empty of this 'independent self' or 'independent nature.' Because everything is interconnected, arises when the conditions are right (Dependent Origination), and all things ("we"/"self") are a temporary grouping due to causes and conditions and will eventually cease existing in that current form, everything is therefore 'empty' of a permanent, unchanging 'self' which does not really exist.

- **Enlightenment:** When one has eliminated all obstructions of the mind, perfected insight and wisdom, and abandoned defilements, they are liberated from the cycle of rebirth and enter the state of Nirvāṇa. While the different Buddhist traditions define enlightenment differently, Theravāda views the Arhat as the ideal. In contrast, Mahāyāna views the Bodhisattva as the ideal as they strive to become a Buddha (Bodhisattva path).

- **Five Precepts:** Abstaining from killing living beings, theft, sexual misconduct, speaking lies/falsehood, and intoxication.

- **Five Skandhas / Aggregates:** The Five Aggregates, also referred to as the Five Skandhas, refers to the temporary, ever-changing conditions that make up a sentient being, such as a human or cat. The first of the Five Aggregates, matter, is also known as "Rupa" or "Body." The other four are "Nama" or "Mind." Together, they are known as "Namarupa," which is a formation of our "store consciousness" (Alayavijnana), ourselves, and our environment. Sentient beings believe they have an independent and permanent self, which causes suffering (Dukkha) in their lives and the cycle of rebirth. The teaching of the Five Aggregates helps a Buddhist understand they are a temporary grouping of things that arise when the conditions are right (birth) and cease in the future (death).

- **Four Noble Truths:** The Four Noble Truths are the Buddha's explanation (as if he were a Doctor) of the disease, the cause of the disease, the prognosis, and the cure for what ails all sentient beings. This "ailment" is known as Dukkha (commonly referred to as "suffering" but has a deeper meaning related to the fundamental unsatisfactoriness and painfulness of mundane life) and affects us at various times in our life.

- **Heart Sutra:** One of the shortest and most recited scriptures in Mahāyāna Buddhism regarding the perfection of wisdom is called Prajna Paramita. One is to take the sutra into the heart and uncover its true meaning through practice. Intellect, analysis, and faith alone will not be enough to understand the sutra.

- **Karma:** The word "Karma" means "deed" or "action" in the ancient Sanskrit language and is a core teaching in all schools of Buddhism. Karma (Kamma in Pāli) governs the concept of "cause and effect," meaning that all "intentional" actions produce results that the doer ("you") will eventually feel. Any "good deeds" would receive positive (wholesome) karmic effects, and any "bad deeds" would produce negative (unwholesome) karmic results. Karma also exists with other types of sentient beings, communities, countries, and even the earth. There are three types of Karma identified by the Buddha: Karma generated by the body (your actions), Karma caused by speech (your words), and Karma developed by the mind (your thoughts).

- **Karmic Actions:** Any actions you intentionally do with your body, speech, or mind will create karmic results. *Wholesome* karmic actions are based upon generosity, compassion, kindness, sympathy, mindfulness, or wisdom. *Unwholesome* karmic actions are based upon greed, hatred, and delusion. *Neutral* (or "Ineffective") karmic actions have no impact and include unintentional activities such as sleeping, breathing, eating, unintentionally stepping on an ant, etc.

- **Mahāyāna:** One of the two major branches of Buddhism currently in practice today and has many 'sects' or traditions within it in the east-Asian countries of China, Taiwan, Japan, Korea, and Vietnam, and central-Asian countries of Tibet, Himalayas, etc. It asserts that all sentient beings, not just monastics, can realize enlightenment and eventually become a Buddha through following the Bodhisattva path.

- **Mala:** A mala is like prayer beads used in other religions. Different Buddhist traditions use them to count recitations, sūtras, chanting, or even visually to signify the abbot of a monastery. Most lay Buddhists wear a small mala on their wrist to identify themselves as Buddhist.

- **Mantra:** Usually, a sound, word, or saying that is used as a form of meditative concentration or invocation.

- **Māra:** A celestial demon that tempts humans and prevents them from becoming awakened. Māra tried to seduce Prince Siddhārtha as he meditated towards awakening. However, Siddhārtha was able to defeat Māra's actions, and he became the Buddha. Māra is also an analogy for our mind that causes delusion, hatred, and desire.

- **Metta:** Commonly referred to as "Loving Kindness" in Buddhism, it is called Maitrī (Sanskrit) / Mettā (Pāli) and is a popular form of meditation. It is also one of the Ten Pāramitās of Theravāda Buddhism.

- **Monkey Mind:** Human Buddhists often refer to "monkey mind," meaning random thoughts and actions like a monkey in the wild.

- **Nirvāṇa:** The state of being liberated and free of wrong perceptions, delusions, and their causes. Nirvāṇa (Nibbāna in Pāli) is the natural state of all beings where there is a cessation of unsatisfactory conditions and causes. However, most beings are unaware of this natural truth and are trapped in an endless cycle of rebirth.

- **Non-Self:** A central concept that states that there is no unchanging, independent, and permanent 'self,' 'soul,' or 'essence,' of any phenomena. Anātman (Sanskrit) / Anattā (Pāli). Everything is devoid of an individual self, but most beings are unaware of this truth.

- **Ox Herding Pictures:** Illustrations that help to teach Buddhists the Zen/Chán path towards enlightenment. They are also referred to as the "Ten Bulls" pictures.

- **Pali:** One of the scholarly languages used in ancient India. Most notably, it is used as the language of the Pāli Canon of the Theravāda tradition found in Southeast Asia.

- **Patriarch:** In certain Buddhist traditions, such as Zen and Chán, records of historical teachers and their lineage back to the Buddha are kept. This lineage helps to establish that a school's teachings are connected back to the Buddha himself.

- **Prajna Paramita:** Essentially, the perfected way of seeing the true nature of reality. Prajna=Wisdom and Paramita=Perfection. The Prajñāpāramitā also refers to nearly 40 different sūtras in Mahāyāna Buddhism.

- **Pure Land:** In Mahāyāna Buddhism, there are numerous celestial Buddhas who have a *Pure Land* where awakening under their guidance is easily achieved. This is only a temporary place, as one will continue in the cycle of rebirth.

- **Saffron:** A color that is said to have been worn by the Buddha and other early Buddhists. It is now most predominately used for the color of the robes of Buddhist monastics of Theravāda Buddhism in Southeast Asia. Buddhist monastics of other traditions wear similarly colored robes, although not the exact same saffron color.

- **Samatha Meditation:** Samatha Meditation is essentially to "calm" or "settle" the mind of random thoughts.

- **Saṃsāra:** The cycle of rebirth, where birth, mundane existence, then death, are repeated endlessly and uncontrollably. This cycle is not comfortable and results in Duḥkha. One who is awakened and realizes enlightenment frees themselves from Saṃsāra and lives in their natural state of Nirvāṇa.

- **Sangha:** The community of ordained Buddhist monastics (monks and nuns). It may also be used to refer to the community of Buddhist practitioners.

- **Sanskrit:** One of the scholarly languages used in ancient India. There were numerous schools of early Buddhism, and many used this language for their scriptural canons. It is now found most notably in the Chinese Canon used by several countries and traditions in East Asian Buddhism. The Mahāyāna Sūtras found in this Canon were initially written in Sanskrit.

- **Sentient Beings:** A living being that has consciousness or sentience. Human beings are sentient beings, whereas a tree would not be.

- **Sutra / Sutta:** A Sūtra (Sanskrit; 'Sutta' in Pāli) is a teaching/sermon of the Buddha. However, it can also be from one of his enlightened disciples or a Bodhisattva.

- **Store Consciousness:** Commonly referred to as the "seed consciousness" or "storehouse consciousness." The Buddhist term is "ālāyavijñāna" (Sanskrit). This is where karmic actions are 'stored' until the right conditions arise so they can come to fruition.

67

- **Suffering:** *See "Dukkha" / "Duḥkha"*

- **Theravāda:** One of the two major branches of Buddhism currently in practice today, which is the main religion and Buddhist tradition in the southeast-Asian countries of Sri Lanka, Thailand, Burma, Nepal, Cambodia, and is also part of Vietnamese Buddhism (which also incorporates Mahāyāna's Pure Land and Meditation schools). Theravāda is often differentiated in the fact that it does not recognize, or practice, any of the Mahāyāna sūtras.

- **Venerable:** Monastics (monks or nuns) are often referred to as "Venerable" in Mahāyāna Buddhism. Venerable Master is a title to the high-ranking monk in a Chán (Chinese Buddhism) or Zen (Japanese Buddhism) temple or organization.

- **Vipassana:** Vipassana is the *result* of meditation (*insight*); however, it is now a type of modern meditation practice. For humans, after we calm our mind (Samatha), insight meditation (analytical) is essential to understand the world we live in and about ourselves.

- **Vultures Peak:** A famous place in Buddhist history where the Buddha taught numerous times.

- **Zen / Chán:** A tradition of Mahāyāna Buddhism practiced in several east-Asian countries, which focuses primarily on meditation. Originally from China, where it is known as Chán, thanks to the teachings of the wandering monk *Bodhidharma*. Chán has since spread to Japan (*Zen*), Korea (*Seon*), and Vietnam (*Thiền*).

Find additional glossary items online:
https://alanpeto.com/buddhism/buddhist-glossary/

Your Notes

About the Authors

Los Angeles Sanathavihari Bhikkhu (Ricardo Ortega) is a Mexican-American Theravāda resident monk at the *Sarathchandra Buddhist Center* in North Hollywood, California (Sri Lankan Buddhist tradition). He is a student of the late *Bhante Punnaji*, and the director of *Casa De Bhavana* - an outreach project to bring the Dhamma to the Spanish-speaking world. He is a regular contributor to *Buddhist Door Global in Español* and has appeared in the Buddhist magazines *Lions Roar* and *Buddhadharma*. B.A. in Religion. U.S. Air Force veteran. **https://www.casadebhavana.com**

Alan Peto is a Mahāyāna layperson in the tradition of *Humanistic Buddhism* with the *Fo Guang Shan (FGS)* Buddhist Order founded by *Venerable Master Hsing Yun* and given the Dharma name *Pu Li*. His Dharma Temple is *Hsi Lai* located in Los Angeles County, California. He is an author and content creator who helps Westerners and beginners understand Buddhism from the layperson perspective. U.S. Navy veteran. **https://alanpeto.com**

75

Printed in Great Britain
by Amazon

48451260R00046